1

Animals were food for the First People. They hunted animals on land and on the water.

**3**

Ducks were hunted for food. The ducks were caught by the feet. The hunter swam under the ducks.

**5**

Canoes were used for hunting on water. They could spear fish from the canoe.

7

Turtles were hunted. Turtles were caught by jumping on to them.

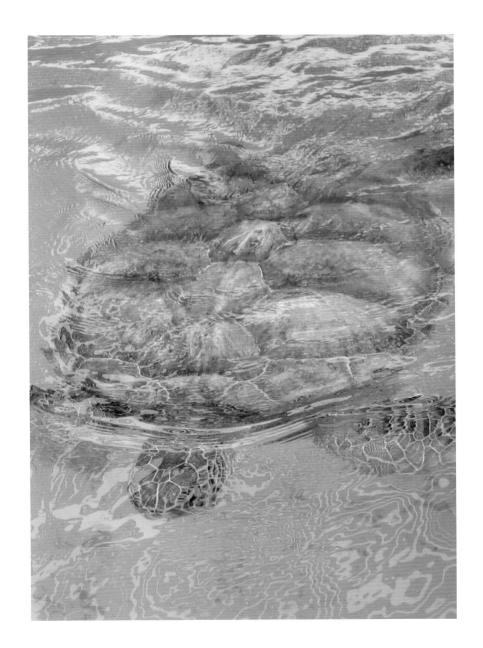

**9**

Goannas were hunted. It was very good food. The goanna has sharp claws and can bite.

**11**

Inside trees were grubs. The First People would eat these grubs.

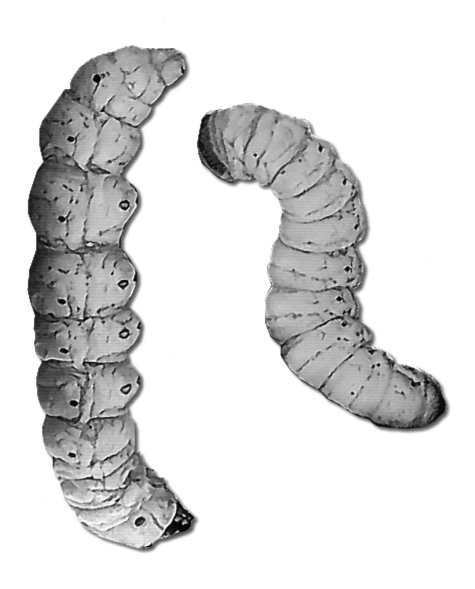

**13**

Bees in Australia make honey.
Beehives were found in trees
and rocks.

**15**

Eggs were a very good food. All birds lay eggs. Eggs were found in nests.

**17**

Fires were lit to chase animals. The animals would jump away from the fire. The hunter would spear the animals.

**19**

Dugongs live in warm waters of Australia. Dugongs were hunted for food. They hunted dugongs from canoes using spears.

**21**

Fires were used to burn grasslands. Animals came to eat the new grass and were hunted for food.

**23**

# Word bank

nests

beehive

animals

hunting

caught

hunter

canoes

speared

turtles

jumping

goanna

grubs

people

dugongs

grasslands